(fail not)

(fail not) A guide to success for teens and young adults

© Copyright 2011, Three Spirits Press, LLC

ISBN: 978-0-9760304-2-3
Library of Congress Card Number: 2010938705

Written by Alan Lohner
Photography: Jason Savage
Design: Cory Raff

Visit our website at www.ThreeSpiritsPress.com
for more information on (fail not) and other
books of higher purpose.

Printed in Canada

We dedicate (fail not) in honor of the following men, women, and children:

Alejandro
Merwin Anderson
Mildred Anderson
Thomas Martin Arnold
Sunida Austin
Jordan Baker
Rita Baller
Ray Berger
Susan Berger
Lily Bohl
Cam Boscole
Laura Boscole
Madison Boscole
Phillip Boscole
Chris Brinkly
Susan Bruner
Melinda Bynum
Landa Carlson
Mary Beth Carnaghan
Amanda Leigh Coffenberry
Neil E. Cronin
Cameron Crowley
Erin Crowley
Judith Crowley
Grant Cumpston
Jeff Cumpston
James Dauber
Laurie Daven
Anthony "Tony" Dostal
Allison Engelstad
Mark Engelstad
Dominique Forrest
Teresa Francione

Greg Galeski
Frances Speight Gaul
Carolyn Givens
Jerry Gloster
Julio Granda
Ralph Henschen
Dan Hoering
Jeff Hoering
Rita M. Hoering
Connor Hollenbeck
James R. Hollenbeck
Joel Hootman
Zong "Grandpa" Hsiang
Alexas Johnson
Scott Jones
Michele Killian
Laura Kleemann
John Lane
Alan Craig Lohner, Jr.
James Joseph Lohner
John Christopher Lohner
Joseph Michael Lohner
Ryan Lopez
Yusuf Mahmoud
Richard McQuillin
John Meyers
Katharine Meyers
Ruth Meyers
William Meyers
Dominic Monterossi
Donovan Mark Nelson
Tara Trabosh Niemann
Emily Noreen
Naomi Noreen

Tyler Noreen
Max G. Papazian
Stephen Perfect
Ryan Peterson
Brian Piercy
Allison Popovich
Paige Popovich
Sharon Quesset
Britany Redfield
Alexander Robinson
Debbie Robinson
Bette Savage
Vada Lynn Schneider
Jim Sheridan
Mary Sheridan
Mary A. Shirley
Diane Siegrist
Gus Siegrist
Peggy Speight
Rosemary Stallbaumer
Brittany Stigen
Robert Quentin Strong
John J. Trabosh
Victoria H. Trabosh
John D. Walker
David Howard Warner
Robert Warner
Ila Welburn
Daryl Welch
Debra Welch
Willis L. Winter
Jane Yost
Wallace Yost

Believe that
you deserve the best.

Your pathway to success begins

with a basic belief: you are worthy of love,

a rewarding career, and a long and happy life.

(fail not) suggests ways to boost your self-image,

while encouraging you to let go of things that

are beyond your control. Anything is possible

if you practice staying positive and

follow your heart.

Put the past ahead of you.

Whatever happened yesterday can't bother
you unless you let it. Look for positive lessons
from everything, no matter how challenging
this seems. Push aside disappointment
and regret with new beginnings and
new possibilities.

Question all
you've been taught.

Accept nothing as it appears and keep
a curious open mind. Find your own truth
by searching, questioning, and experiencing.
Go beyond the mainstream media,
where information is often suppressed or
altered by bias and special interests,
and seek out other sources of news
and facts.

You're gonna screw up.

You aren't perfect and your life isn't
going to be perfect. When you make mistakes,
learn from them, don't be too hard on yourself,
and don't allow others to hurt your self-image.
Rather than dwell on any one mistake,
concentrate on solutions, make amends if need
be, and think forward, not backward.

Set unrealistic goals.

Be bold in your ambitions, because greatness
emerges from wild imaginings. Write down your
goals, and break them down into action items
that you can track. Stay flexible, because some
changes will naturally occur, but don't lose
sight of your major objectives.

Be still.

Make time every day to relax and quiet
your mind. During this time, let go of anything
that's bothering you. Spending peaceful time
alone brings insights that can enlighten
and inspire you.

Learning
isn't about grades.

Fixating on your grade-point average
takes the purpose and enjoyment out of
learning. Balance school work with other activities,
including sports, music, a part-time job,
or volunteering. Getting a well-rounded
education requires gaining life experience
outside of a classroom.

People are talking behind your back.

So what? There will always be people who don't like you or don't understand you. Worrying about it only diminishes your power and peace of mind.

Dare to differ.

Peer pressure may push you to follow a
crowd to gain acceptance. However, the only
person who needs to accept you is you.
By exercising self-discipline and staying true
to yourself, you'll earn the admiration
of others, even though they may not
admit it or show it.

Rely on
your intuitive powers.

While rational thought is a valuable
asset in making decisions, it is also important
to trust your own inner voice. The material
world can hinder you from becoming fully
aware of all that is. Your mind and heart
know no physical limits, and by practicing
meditation and prayer, valuable information
will come to you.

No one is normal.

Society attempts to force conformity
on everyone. Resist this and follow your
own inner compass. "Normal" is a purely
subjective term and no one is perfect or
knows all the answers.

Give thanks for nothing.

Try to appreciate everything you have,
even on days when you feel everything is
going against you. Get in the habit of saying
"thank you" for little things, because nothing
is unimportant. Gratitude lifts the mood
of those around you, helps cancel
negative thinking, and attracts more
good things into your life.

You won't find yourself in a mirror.

Your true self goes way beyond what you can see. Looks don't last. What you offer the world has everything to do with dedication and commitment and less to do with outward appearances.

Celebrities and athletes are just people.

It is good to have role models and
to admire the achievements of others.
Remember, though, that famous people have
the same strengths and weaknesses as anyone.
Many heroes have everyday jobs and will
never know fame or fortune.

You are not responsible for your parents' relationship.

Divorce and separation can be painful,
especially if you believe you're somehow at fault
for what's happened. Your parents' relationship
is their responsibility, though, and you aren't
to blame for their breakup. Talk to people
you trust—friends, counselors, or clergy—
and don't keep self-defeating thoughts
to yourself.

(fail not)
to be patient.

Achievements, both great and small,
take time to bring about. Expecting too
much too soon prevents you from appreciating
incremental successes. Find contentment
in the here and now, because impatience
makes you lose sight of the present,
throwing you off track.

Waste nothing.

Every waking moment need not be
filled with tasks and accomplishment,
but let this serve as a reminder that every day
is a gift. As such, take care not to waste
resources or opportunities. The importance
of making full use of your time and
talents cannot be overstated.

Real euphoria
transcends any drug.

Artificial stimulants are just that—artificial. Self-medication and escapism are only temporary and will not make you happy in the long run. Finding a connection to life outshines any and all drugs.

Find victory in defeat.

It's always more fun to win, but you learn more when you lose. Accept responsibility for your role in any defeat, and learn how mistakes can help you grow stronger. When you view setbacks from a different point of view, you position yourself for eventual success.

Love isn't sex.

Sex is physical; love is spiritual.

You don't need sexual contact to love another.

True love is patient, kind, unconditional,

and undemanding.

Be popular
with yourself.

You may feel it's all-important to be liked
by others, but it's most important to like yourself.
Learn how to be your own best friend by
accepting yourself as you are and focusing on the
good that is within you. Make wise choices,
especially if others try to lead you away from your
own inner guidance, and you will earn the most
satisfying reward of all—self-respect.

Talk back.

It's okay to ask parents and authority
figures to explain rules that you disagree with.
Try to understand the reasoning behind anything
that limits you, and discuss your feelings openly.
Learning how to communicate effectively and
respectfully is an important skill that will
benefit you the rest of your life.

Believe in
what you can't see.

You possess a source of inner knowing
that transcends time and space. The pleasures
and pain of this world are deceptive and fleeting.
But always know that your mind and spirit
survive the physical world.

College isn't for everyone.

Earning a college education provides
real advantages. However, there are many
beneficial and practical paths for higher learning.
Trade schools, apprenticeships, traveling abroad,
or finding an entry-level job all deserve
consideration, depending on your goals
and abilities.

You will see departed loved ones again.

Do not despair too deeply over the death of someone you love. Grief is fitting, a natural process of letting go, but remember that you will reconnect with loved ones at a future time. Honor those who have passed before you by undertaking productive tasks during your days on earth.

Suicide erases your best options.

If you think about ending your life, be aware there is another part of you—your spirit—that will not die. There are many unhappy consequences of suicide for those left behind, and you may discover even more challenging lessons facing you on the other side. You are encouraged to seek and find the unconditional love, support, and help that exist here and now, on this side, because it is the best way for you to learn that life goes in cycles— both pleasant and difficult—and that it is definitely possible for you to feel better.

Guilt does you no good.

Beating yourself up over something doesn't help a situation—it only serves to make you feel worse. When you see that you've made a mistake, look for what you can do to make things right. If you carry around guilt and shame, it will drag you down.

No thing and no other person can make you happy.

Happiness comes from within.
You control your thoughts and how you
react to other people and events is totally
up to you. This is a simple but powerful
truth that can help you each
and every day.

Help!

When you lend a hand to others,
it's all to your benefit. In fact, to get what
you really want, help people get what they need.
You're rewarded by how much and how
selflessly you give.

What you wear
is not who you are.

Avoid judging others by their appearance
or what they wear. A person's worth goes far
beyond style and designer imprints.
Nice clothes are just nice clothes.

(fail not)
to persevere.

Succeeding at anything requires
commitment, a belief in yourself, and a
steadfast attitude. Strike the words
"I can't" from your vocabulary.
Never lose faith, never lose hope,
and never give up.

Forgive and find peace.

Few directives in life are so simple,
yet so challenging. Revenge seems to satisfy,
but it is a trick, and offers no lasting healing.
Practicing forgiveness is extremely hard, but it
is the only sure path to personal peace.

The best schooling
isn't in school.

If you limit your learning to the classroom,
you're missing out on invaluable life lessons.
Get involved in activities outside of school
through sports, work, hobbies, spiritual practice,
volunteering, and interacting with a wide variety
of different people. What you experience in
the world stays with you far longer than
what you read in a book.

Your career choice belongs to you.

You may feel that you must please your parents, friends, or counselors in the career path you choose. However, the responsibility for your career rests solely with you. Follow your passion—regardless of the financial aspects—because if you love your work, you'll more than likely do well at it.

Serving others
serves you.

Make an effort to make a difference in
your community. Volunteer at a senior center
or retirement home, become active in your
church or local youth group, befriend a neighbor
in need, or participate in school activities.
Do whatever you can to help people, and it
will come back to you in a good way.

Death does not end life.

Life goes on outside of your body,

because your spirit is immortal. Knowing this

gives you freedom to live life fully. Make healthy

decisions and expect to live for many years,

so you can learn as much as you can in

the physical form.

Love the unloved.

Be nice to everyone, especially those
less fortunate than you, because you never
know how much your words and actions can
end up helping or hurting someone. If you
belittle, ridicule, or bully, you're not only injuring
another, you're also creating more problems
for yourself, because bad behavior leads to
bad outcomes. If you're the victim of bullying,
tell people you trust what's going on,
and be persistent until concrete steps are
taken to stop it.

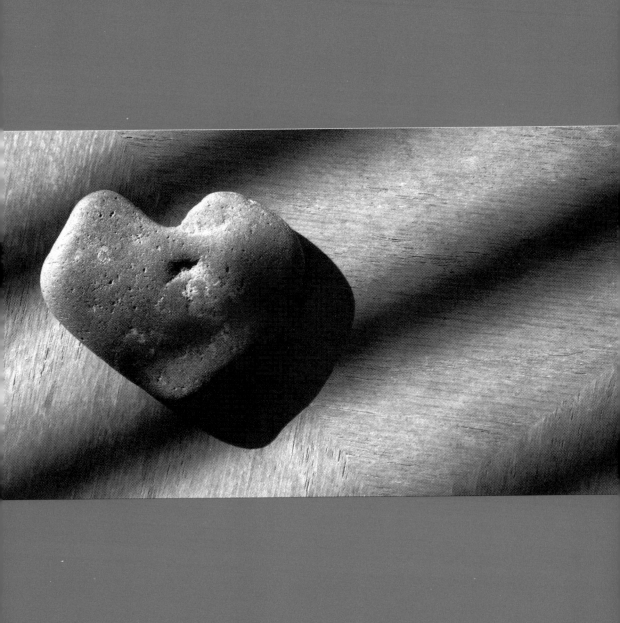

Sweat.

Make exercise a regular part of your day.
It's a habit that will benefit you all of your life.
Find something you enjoy—running,
hiking, swimming, or playing a sport—
and stick with it.

No one else's beliefs can hurt you.

You can always control what
you're thinking. So in a very real sense,
only you can bring pain or peace to your life.
Once you master this simple concept,
you'll see that it's possible to choose
healing over hurt, even in the most
trying circumstances.

Act your age.

In other words, run and jump,
sing and dance, laugh and play. The world
is challenging, complex, and unpredictable.
Balance life's uncertainties with humor,
exuberance, and positive thinking.

Love hurts
as much as you let it.

Feeling pain because a relationship has
gone bad is natural. You can lessen the hurt by
letting go of unrealistic attachment and desire.
If you can practice unconditional love and wish
happiness for others regardless of what they do,
you will help yourself feel better sooner.

Travel and grow.

You can only experience so much
by remaining in the same surroundings.
One of the best ways to learn about yourself
and put your life in sharper perspective is
to travel, when you have the opportunity.
By connecting with others from different
places, you gain a greater appreciation for
the world and your importance in it.

Take heart
from hardship.

Search for a lesson in whatever happens
in your life. Tough times will make you stronger,
although it's hard to see benefits when going
through a personal trial. When you face adversity
head-on and take action to overcome it,
you boost your self-confidence, which further
empowers you to succeed.

Drive like
your life depends on it.

Know the speed limit and maintain it,
especially if others encourage you to break it.
Try not to get angry, even when another driver
does something stupid. Refuse to ride in any
vehicle that's driven by someone who's
impaired by drugs or alcohol.

Use words wisely.

Whatever you say, whether written or spoken,
is helpful or harmful. Angry words are especially
damaging, not only to others but also to yourself.
Conversely, words of kindness create unlimited
opportunities for growth, understanding,
and healing.

(fail not)
to stay positive.

Life challenges you constantly. In every
situation, keep a positive outlook and expect
that you will overcome any obstacle.
Get in the habit of asking others for help,
because this is a sign of strength and shows
that you care about yourself.

Turn it up.

Listen to what you enjoy—anything that
connects with you. Whatever you may be
experiencing or feeling, chances are someone has
written a song about it, and it's out there for you
to discover. Let music calm you, inspire you,
and energize you.

Befriend an enemy.

Holding a grudge against someone else
is harmful to both of you. One small act of
kindness or compassion can make a big
difference toward healing a strained relationship.
Offering a hand in forgiveness is a sign of
inner strength, not weakness.

See yourself as successful.

Imagine what you want your life to be,
and picture it in your mind. Do this as often as
you can, and your imaginings will become
increasingly real—and attainable. It's a natural
fact—when you focus on something good,
it gives you the mental strength to make
it happen.

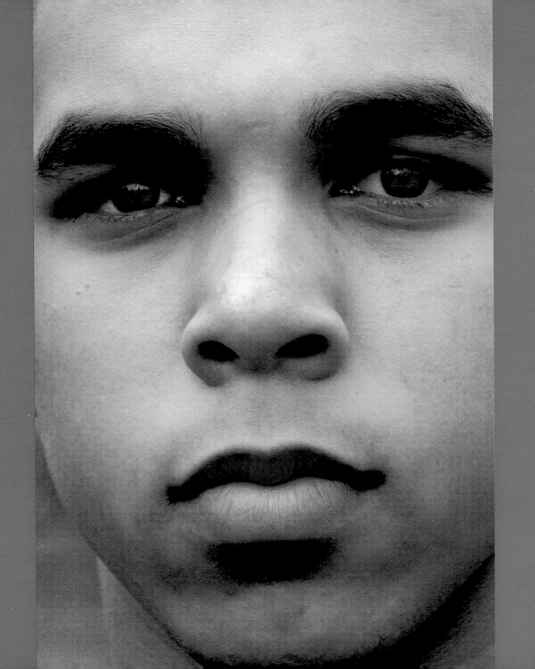

Setbacks are stepping stones.

No one ever achieved great success
without stumbling many times along the way.
The more often you "fail" the more you learn,
so embrace challenges, no matter how daunting
they may appear. Remember to be patient,
persevere, and stay positive.

You can change the world.

People just like you have done
amazing things. If you have a big idea,
act on it. Your passion and enthusiasm
can inspire others to follow you.

Sex isn't love.

Sex joins bodies, but love connects
on a much deeper level. Someone who really
cares about you will not pressure you into
having sex. Engaging in sexual activity before
you're ready creates more challenges
than solutions.

Anyone can drink.

You can probably deceive others and find
a way to drink alcohol, even if you're underage.
The question is: how intelligent are you about
the consequences of drinking? You are responsible
for everything you do, and if you are under the
influence of alcohol, you severely impair your
ability to think, act, and make the best
choices for yourself.

No body is perfect.

Those beautiful images of models that you see in the media are just that—images that have been doctored to look "perfect." Every body has imperfections, so take care not to overdo exercise or dieting in the pursuit of perfection—it's an impossible quest. How your body works on the inside is much more important than how it looks outside.

Remember your veggies.

Good physical and mental health is
a precious gift. Respect that gift by making
smart choices about what you eat and drink.
By doing so, you'll give yourself the greatest
chance to be your absolute best in mind,
body, and spirit.

You are never alone.

Even when you feel isolated and confused,
you are connected to an unlimited source of
spiritual guidance and love. Tapping into
this source requires an open mind and
quiet reflection. What you can sense is as
real as what you can see.

Let insults inspire you.

When others attack you with words,
they are actually demonstrating hurtful things
about themselves. If you really think about it,
any angry outburst stems from fear and
weakness. By understanding this, you can see
insults in a different light, and you'll be less
likely to be affected by them.

You are
here for a reason.

Even though the world often seems chaotic,
everyone and everything has order, purpose,
and a reason for being. Knowing this brings
comfort but also carries responsibility.
You were born to fulfill a mission in the
universe's grand scheme.

Asking for help
gives you power.

If you feel angry, afraid, sad, or confused
about something, go to someone you trust and
talk about it. Asking for help is hard, but once
you do it, you give yourself more options and
more peace of mind. When you reach out to a
friend, family member, or counselor, it enables
you to release difficult emotions, find resolutions,
and see new possibilities.

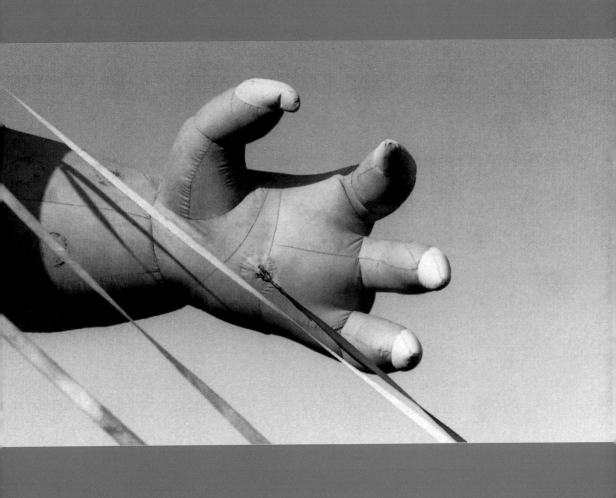

Blame nothing
or no one.

When things go wrong, it's natural to
want to point a finger at others. Avoid this
practice, because it leads to more
negative outcomes. Instead, take responsibility
for your role in any disappointment and
you'll better understand which corrective
measures will work.

Create the
life you want.

Hold a vision for your future.
Respect and nurture it. Let no one—
or no circumstance—stand in the way
of your dreams.

(fail not) A guide to success for teens and young adults is the second book in Alan Lohner's "Exalted Living Series" from Three Spirits Press. The first book in the series, *(fear not) Venture to inner peace*, has been acclaimed around the world for its healing words and images.

Back in the late 1970s, Alan served as a patrolman in his hometown of Toledo, Ohio, where he witnessed the tragedy of murders, suicides, and traffic fatalities. He was the first person on the scene when his brother John was killed in a single-car accident.

Alan was visited by John in a dream about 40 nights after his death. During that visitation, Alan was told specific information on various topics: caring spirits watch over us, waste is frowned upon, free will requires responsibility, children who pass away are master teachers, death is merely a doorway into another life, and we will see departed loved ones again.

In August 2002, on the eighth anniversary of his mother's death, Alan was visited by three spirit guides who pointedly instructed him: it's counterproductive to squander time and energy, be true to yourself and others, and connect with everything.

The wisdom that Alan received during these visitations—and truths he has uncovered on his own spiritual journey—have been woven into *(fear not)* and *(fail not)*.

About the author:

Alan Lohner has been writing professionally for nearly 30 years, and he earned a master's degree in journalism from the University of Oregon. His first book, *(fear not) Venture to inner peace*, has positively impacted people on every continent. He lives in suburban Portland, Oregon with his two sons, Alan Jr. and Joseph, their two pet dachshunds, Rocky and Howard, and their adopted cat, Stormy.

About the photographer:

Jason Savage has an uncanny talent for capturing the offbeat and dramatic behind his photo lens. He finds inspiration for his photos from real life, as well as every other art medium. In 2003, Jason relocated from Indiana to Portland, Oregon, where he enjoys exploring all the wonders of the Pacific Northwest.

About the designer:

Cory Raff has more than 25 years of experience in graphic design. He's operated his own advertising and design business since 1985. Cory is a native of Gresham, Oregon and he earned an associate's degree in design at Mount Hood Community College.

Give the gift of empowerment.

Share the inspiring words of (fail not) by purchasing additional copies for friends and family members.

You can order (fail not) online at: ThreeSpiritsPress.com

Or call us toll-free at 866-550-0149.

Inspire others with your story.

If the messages in this book have helped you experience greater fulfillment in your life, we invite you to share your story with other readers in future publications.

Please send an email to: mystory@ThreeSpiritsPress.com

We welcome all comments and suggestions. Send your email to: publisher@ThreeSpiritsPress.com